REFLECTIONS

WITH GLYN EDWARDS

REFLECTIONS

WITH GLYN EDWARDS

Compiled and with additional material by Santoshan (Stephen Wollaston)

Independent Publishing Platform
Distributed and printed by Amazon

First edition
ISBN (13) 978-1080308798 / (10) 1080308792

Design and artwork by Santoshan (Stephen Wollaston)

Cherry blossom cover photo © Christian Musat/Shutterstock.com
Back cover and page 7 photo of Glyn Edwards by Tony Stewart
Page 45 and 46 photo © Rawpixel.com/Shutterstock.com
Page 107 and 108 photo © KMNPhoto/Shutterstock.com
Page 128 photo of Glyn Edwards by Santoshan (Stephen Wollaston)

Contents

Glyn Edwards 1949-2015

Introduction

This book is being released to coincide with what would have been Glyn's 70th Earth-year on 17th August. Like many books, it came about organically, after completing a tribute book I was approached about compiling, celebrating Glyn's life and work, which included a selection of quotations by him. It became a natural step to then think what a book of this kind, with a more comprehensive collection of quotations, might look like. This anthology is obviously the result of those thoughts.

For those who may not know much about him and would like to know more, the tribute book, *Glyn Edwards: A Renowned Medium Remembered*, would be a good place to start. Not wanting to repeat what has already been written for that title, I will give just a brief overview about him in this introduction and will let his own words in the following pages speak for themselves. But before doing so, I should perhaps mention why the cover says 'with additional material by Santoshan'. It is because the bulk of the first book and some parts of the second one that Glyn and I wrote were jointly authored. The References section at the back of this book shows where coauthored passages have been used.

Glyn Edwards

Most people who knew Glyn, saw him work and attended his courses will agree that he was an outstanding teacher, orator and demonstrator of mediumship, with a deep interspiritual, inclusive approach to his wisdom. He personally viewed mediumistic work as a sacred vocation, and frequently promoted numerous other realms of development. He sometimes ran courses and spiritual retreats that did not include mediumship at all, which were just as popular as the ones he ran on mediumistic unfoldment. Students and teachers on his courses and workshops could come from a variety of traditions such as Hindu, Christian, Jewish, Yogic, Buddhist, Sufi, Psychotherapist, Reiki Healer and Neo-Pagan, and could be of any age from teenage years to senior citizens.

His insight into and experience of an array of interrelated realms of spirituality was unquestionably phenomenal and deeply profound. It was through his influence that my own journey opened up to different areas of spirituality and mystical insight, of which I will always be grateful and offer this book in honour of his memory, friendship and encouragement.

On Retreat with Glyn and this Anthology

It was a few days after the great storm of 1990 when a delightful elderly Swami at the Ramakrishna Vedanta Centre in Bourne End informed Glyn and me about using passages for meditative purposes by the following method. However, I have added some preliminary steps and suspect that Glyn may have already been aware of the practice because of his early years in a Benedictine monastery and was probably being polite by not mentioning this at the time.

Glyn himself frequently enjoyed going on spiritual retreats to various countryside and town monasteries in England. With his deep-rooted universal approach to spirituality, he always took a variety of reflective reading material from various mystical and wisdom traditions with him. He found quiet breaks and times of peaceful reflection and contemplative reading profoundly beneficial and healing, and often shared heartfelt feelings and insights during such times.

Compiling and laying out Glyn's wisdom for this anthology, for similar use to the way he himself used spiritual reading in his own development, has been an enjoyable and enriching experience. I can only trust that readers will also find it a valuable and inspiring addition to other titles by him.

Suggestions for How to Use this Book

You may read this book as you wish, of course – if done in the right way, simply reading it straight through can be a form of meditation – but if you require some guidance, you might like to find a peaceful place on your own or with a small group of friends in your home or garden, or in the countryside or a tranquil place of worship. Take time to be still and quieten your mind. Sit in an upright position, with the spine erect. Feel the weight of your body on the chair, cushion or ground you are sitting on. Be aware of your interconnectedness with Gaia, with Mother Earth, with how the plants and trees feed you with life-giving oxygen and in return your breath feeds them. Consciously release any tension in your mind and body by taking a gentle deep breath and feeling it gently flowing into your lungs, noticing your upper-chest and abdomen rising naturally, and when you breathe out, slowly and gently exhale and release any tension with the out-breath. Set the intension of seeking to be one with the spirit world and in harmony with all that is within and around you.

Now allow your breathing to find its own natural rhythm. Select one of the passages you feel drawn to in this book, or open it randomly on a page. Read the passage slowly. If you are with friends, select one amongst you to read a passage aloud. Reflect upon what the words mean to you. Be with your reflective thoughts and feelings for a while and see what arises with a sense of open-hearted receptiveness. Take your time doing this. You may feel the need to read the passage again and to repeat some of the above steps. You may also wish to reflect upon other passages in this book during this time.

If you are doing this with friends, you will probably want to share any reflective thoughts or feelings that came to you. If on your own, you may wish to write them down in a spiritual journal and come back to what you write for further reflection another time.

All of the above can be done as an exercise in itself, as a preliminary step for another type of practice or part of a day of various contemplative exercises. Traditionally, in contemplative Christian spirituality, a short passage of scripture is often reflected upon for the purpose of awakening to mystical union with the Divine, which is popularly known as *Lectio Divina*, Divine reading, in the Christian tradition. But the practice is also found in other paths, of course. As previously mentioned, it was a Hindu swami who first taught me about it.

~ Santoshan (Stephen Wollaston)

Awakening

1

Life on Mother Earth is not a negative place that
we feel we would be only too pleased to escape.
Its beauty inspires awe and wonder
and has great healing qualities.

In the beginning it may not be clear that
changes are starting to happen.
But with patience and openness
we begin to see where our previous patterns of
thought end and another realm of
understanding and activity is starting to
unfold and guide us.

It's not so much where we are going
or speculating on metaphysical notions
that are of prime importance ~ as there must surely be
levels beyond our understanding ~ but where we are now,
how we respond to life, the Earth, Nature and others
and manifest the reality of our truths
in everyday experience.

By awakening to spiritual dimensions of life,
we have the capacity to become more centred and loving.
In place of limitations
we open ourselves to joy and freedom
and embrace life in compassionate ways.

Living by spiritual laws means going beyond ordinary laws, taking responsibility for every area of our lives ~ our thoughts, feelings and actions ~ and being respectful of everyone and every form of life with which we come into contact.
We may not be able to accomplish this overnight, but it is in the trying that we become more caring, loving, centred, responsible and empowered spiritual beings.

The deeper we are able to go with
the natural flow of our unfoldment
and awaken to the presence of the spirit,
we discover more ways of opening to an array
of spiritual, psychic and mediumistic powers
that we possess.

What can often seem like wrong turns,
false starts or mistakes might discourage us.
But invariably these things help us to
refine our awareness and lead us to
firmer convictions about the paths
we must tread.

As new awareness reveals itself, you will realise new truths. The life you may have lived so far might even come into conflict with fresher and wider fields of vision that require time to integrate before finding harmonious balance.

Our mind and conscious awareness perceive all things as psychic images, sensations, energies and vibrations, which then influence us and express themselves in and through our being.

Through the unfoldment of internal awareness we can awaken to qualities of our true spirit Self, bring down any barriers that we may have created around our hearts and become more in tune with life around us.

We need to cultivate an understanding and
a state of being that accepts and loves others and ourselves
and realise that our true nature is endeavouring to
help us to awaken to the reality of what spirituality is
and how to live deeply and skilfully by it
in every moment.

Through searching we come to ask the age-old questions: "Who am I?", "What am I?", "Why am I here?", "Where am I going?" and "What is creating the appearance of separation from my authentic spiritual nature?" Such questions lead us to a discovery of our greatest qualities of love, compassion, kindness and unity with all things, life, people and species.

Do you have the courage to awaken to and live this radical vision and the truth that can set you free? Spiritual empowerment is in the discovery of who we truly are, which includes the deepest implications for spiritual living.

Seeing into the nature of all things,

I awaken to a life of truth and openness.

The Whole Self

2

It is by healthily awakening to
the various forces within our life
that all areas of existence
become integral parts of
a spiritual whole.

We must remember that
not only our inner senses ~ mediumistic, psychic
and spiritual ~ but that our physical senses
which have wondrously taken millions of
years to evolve are equally valid,
as spirituality is not an escape from one world
into another but an inclusion of
the whole of life.

[O]ur true spirit Self is whole and without boundaries,
and continually seeks to express this wholeness
and boundless nature in and through every level
of our being and everything that we do.
It knows no limitations and has the power to
bring about positive changes, congruence in the ways we
think, feel and act and enhance all creative abilities and
qualities of compassion we have.

The more we know ourselves,
the more we transform ourselves
and the more the spirit world flows
naturally through and within us.

Those who are open and inclusive
in the paths they tread, will find more areas of
their lives receptive to unfoldment and
will take part in the spirit's work in
more fruitful ways.

As we enter into development with an open mind
and a willingness to grow into spiritual maturity,
which means including the inevitable difficulties
and suffering we and others encounter,
along with blissful moments of awakening to divinity,
we begin to realise that all life is ultimately One ~ that
there is no clear division between set systems of belief
or everyday life and spiritual understanding.

Growing

3

In the past we may have been influenced in
our thinking by the beliefs of others.
Now we must take the opportunity to
discover for ourselves their truth
or falsehood.

To maintain spiritual progress we need to go beyond ordinary concentration, to levels where the mind and consciousness are brought in tune and influenced by our spiritual nature in order to bring about changes in the whole of our being.

It is through recognition, receptivity, opening our minds and working with our potential that an awareness of there being no limit to the inherent abilities we have comes into being.

Spiritual empowerment entails
awareness of who and what we are.
It encompasses awareness of our
everyday psychological and spiritual selves
and finding ways of bringing both
into balance with one another.

When we become more open to life,
we heighten our abilities to become more
sensitively aware of all things within and around us.
This, if we are open to allowing it to happen,
can then lead us into realms of change and transformation
~ to embracing who we truly are and
ways in which we can wholesomely grow.

Ultimately, unfoldment leads us to

our authentic nature...

Through the cultivation of open minds and hearts,
we connect more deeply with our true Selves and others,
become in tune with all life and overcome inhibiting
concepts that create barriers to spiritual living.

Allow room for mature growth, wisdom, paradox and the mystery of the unknown, as these will always encourage healthy and wholesome growth.

Unity in Diversity

4

In looking into ourselves for the greatest gifts we possess we discover the gifts of wisdom and Self-knowledge that are the gateways to freedom, true peace and enlightenment. Such things help us to find unity in diversity and the compassionate Spirit in all.

Signs of an authentic spirituality … are found in teachings of inclusiveness, equality, acts of compassion, and honouring different beliefs, insights, practices, ethnicity, sexual orientation and gender.

Spiritual maturity is an essential part of wholesome and skilful growth that needs to be included in our development if we truly wish to progress and move forward in harmony with others.

It is no coincidence that the many spiritual traditions of the world have adopted various uses of prayers, chants, mantras and affirmations. Each can affect and help us in different ways; each have their own value if used correctly.

We must embrace the Light that shines through
other faiths, other ways of thinking and traditions.
An open mind to others is essential.

Diverse as teachings of spirituality may seem, there are always many threads of common ground to be found. When we examine people's search for spiritual dimensions of life, we are looking at their quests to find eternal truths. In understanding the teachings of the world, we come to appreciate many cultures and various ways in which we can grow and realise our true nature.

In various traditions …
[the *universal* spirit] is described in different ways:
in Buddhism as recognising ever-present Buddha Nature;
in Judaism as *ruach*, the spirit and the breath of life;
in Hinduism as the *atman*, the spark of divinity in all;
and in Christianity as the Divine indwelling
and the Cosmic Christ.

I feel it is important that we embrace the light that
is there in numerous spiritual traditions,
and realise that nationality, spiritual background or
beliefs have nothing to do with the phenomena of
mediumistic and psychic powers,
as they are a natural part of everyone's being
and found manifesting in the majority, if not all, of the
world's great wisdom and mystical traditions.

Mediumistic Attunement

5

The subject of mediumistic and psychic powers is, in fact, multifaceted. Including, that when we talk to another person in the physical world we are in fact communicating with another spirit personality because of the spirit that exists in all people, species and things.

If we allow it, the mediumistic journey … opens us to infinite possibilities of growth.

Through mediumistic experience we discover knowledge of another life from which we came and to which we will return.

In my own understanding, mediumship is not about seeking to be a particular type of medium. It is a journey and awakening through numerous spheres of activity and experience that assist us in being more openly receptive to infinite positive potential, and allowing that potential to surface and shine more purely and unrestrictively through all that we do and are.

If we embrace mediumship along with unitive perspectives that look for the best in all of us, they may ultimately guide us to seeing everyone as mediumistic in one way or another and as a member of our global family because of our shared origins and everyone's ability to be aware of the *universal* Spirit in physical form.

We must look at life from all levels.
And within mediumistic unfoldment,
look for not only what can be described as provable facts
but for what can also be included and encouraged for
the purpose of holistic and wholesome growth.

At its deepest level,
the act of mediumship seeks to enhance our daily life
and helps us to be of selfless service to others.

When approached in a healthy way we discover that mediumistic unfoldment is an active and evolving path that leads to new and profound experience and deep contact with the world of the spirit.

The spirit world requires us to get ourselves, our mind, feelings, aspirations and life in tune with one another and settled before working mediumistically.

In mediumistic unfoldment,
as an awareness of the spirit world becomes more
predominant, various spirit influences will be seen
blending with our consciousness.
Yet it is still our choice to what extent we
allow this to happen, how much we open ourselves to
the spirit's influence and embrace wider states
of awareness.

An authentic trust in the spirit is about embracing
the beginning of a deep friendship between yourself and
the invisible world of those that work with you.
This trust is an evolving experience that builds over time
and through the experiences you undergo.
But the most import ingredient of trust,
is trust in yourself and your abilities.

Spirit communication seeks to prove
to humanity that all life survives death.
It seeks to encourage us to reflect upon life,
upon our beliefs and actions and
take responsibility for the evolution of
our spiritual nature.

The more skilled we are in being aware of different levels of being and the changes that take place during mediumistic work, the more open we will be to the spirit's influence and numerous experiences and realms of unfoldment.

Those searching to understand mediumistic awareness and how to communicate better with the spirit world, need to realise that ultimately the answers to unfoldment are to be found within themselves.

If we accept there is a part of us that never dies, then we need to integrate this knowledge into our lives, investigate its implications and establish greater awareness of its reality in our unfoldment.

Honour your mediumistic growth as something sacred that can help and encourage you, other people, life, and the spirit world to manifest and express their love and wisdom more fully in the world.

Creativity

6

Behind all there is that which is creative,
the same Spirit in all, which has imbued all life with
the ability to express its creativity, to become co-creators,
and has allowed humanity to discover life's true purpose
and meaning ~ that ultimately everything is ruled by love
and that our true nature is ultimately loving.

In the course of my development I have come to
realise how our individual spirit, Nature,
the spirit world and God are continuously creating,
and how by participating with this activity we become
co-creators with the creative powers of all life.

The underlying teachings of the spirit are about awakening to the Oneness of all life and becoming co-creators with the spirit and the Divine expressing their creativity.

All we need to do is be responsive to
positive growth and willing to be more
active instruments for the compassionate
and creative work of the spirit.

Goodness and creativity
flow in me, through me and from me.
I am a part of the creative force
that works in and through all life.
As this power is an intrinsic part of who I am,
I claim a life of continuous and eternal growth.
I accept and acknowledge my good and my creative
spiritual potential and continually work towards
expressing them fully in my life.

And by embracing the wondrous creative unity of life, comes a heightened awareness of the presence of the spirit and the Divine revealing themselves in and through all things.

Anything that separates us from others
means separating ourselves from life and
the awe inspiring creativity of God and spirit
working through all.

I realise that all is part of the Divine and that the Divine is expressing its creativity through all.

Interconnectedness

7

[I]f all is interrelated,
we cannot consider the suffering of others
as being separate from ourselves.

When we awaken to these different
worlds [of unfoldment], we come to realise
the interconnectedness of all,
how all things exist in the Divine and the spirit
and how they are profoundly interwoven.
We realise that life is eternal and never dies.
Such things lead us to a discovery of our
greatest qualities of love, compassion, kindness
and unity with all.

Ultimately there is no true separation between people and other life, either in this life or after physical death. We are essentially one spirit that is without boundaries and interconnected equally with all.

There are problems in trying to distinguish too sharply
between inspirational and intuitive knowledge,
the psychic, the mediumistic and the spiritual,
the prophet and the activist, the mystic and the seer …
All have their origins in our being and are an expression of
an interactive whole …

If we seek to be in harmony
with spiritual dimensions of life,
we need to realise that the spirit knows no boundaries.
Therefore we also need to awaken to a life that
embraces all and overcome any sense of separation
from other species and people.

Whether we realise it or not,
we daily live in a psychic world,
and creative and mediumistic abilities
interconnect with this,
as well as with transforming realms
of spirituality.

By deepening our understanding
we realise that all is interconnected
and are parts of one great ocean of life.

Early indigenous people and shamans were
the first humans to connect with a spirit world
permeating nature and to communicate with
their departed ancestors.
Others have looked towards the more
transcendent areas of spirituality.
Although there are some who have never
completely separated themselves from some
of the early indigenous beliefs and practices,
there are some who have,
which has led to an unhealthy separation
between nature and the spirit.

We need to recognise that there are different ways
in which to approach the many faceted dimensions
of spirituality and be open to numerous areas that can
lead us to healthier states of spiritual being
and embrace the all-ness of what
eternal life is about.

Rise above judgmental thoughts and restrictive projections that separate you from others, as ultimately there are no 'others' as we are all interconnected in the Oneness of spirit.

Spirit

8

Our spirit knows the means of expressing
the light of our authentic being.
We only need to listen to its call
and be inspired by its profound influence.

The intuitive self, the knower that knows the unknown,
the shaman that sees into the vision quest,
the yogi that develops the *siddhis* (miraculous powers),
the seer that sees into the possible,
the sensitive who has the ability to communicate
with many levels of life and with those that we love,
will all come to discover that there are no limitations
to the various powers they possess.
They are all facets of our true spirit Self.

As the infinite Spirit within me knows no boundaries,
there is nothing that I cannot do, face or overcome.
All is in harmony with my life.
I am at peace with all that surrounds me.
I see through all things and recognize
the Divine's presence in the centre of all.

Don't let fear enter your unfoldment,
as there is ultimately nothing to be afraid of.
The world of the spirit will join with you,
and through this blending, you will find many wonderful
and beautiful experiences that will enrich your life
and the great work that lies ahead.

As we develop a deeper response to and understanding of our sensitivity and spiritual and psychic nature, we allow the spirit's presence to manifest more fully in our lives and guide us onto richer planes of being and consciousness.

Communicators in the spirit world
often remind us that we are a deathless,
sacred living spirit and often seek to encourage us to
contemplate the implications of this knowledge
and turn it into wholesome actions
such as caring for all life and people,
including ourselves.

Spiritual teachings often highlight how we are essentially a spirit with a body ~ that we are in fact *already* living in a spirit world ~ and how our perceptions simply need to open in order to discover this truth for ourselves.

The spirit seeks to express itself through our body, mind and feelings in order to influence and harmonise all that we do and are.

All physical life on our planet has been
given birth by Mother Earth.
And within physical life there is
the essence of spirit that has always existed.
It is the animating force of all life, breath,
consciousness, awareness and love.

The spirit within me

houses original goodness.

Evolving

9

There is no end to our evolvement
and the potential within us.
It is only we who limit ourselves with
inhibiting beliefs about our spiritual nature
and inherent gifts.

Life is always about moving on and
evolving in the eternity of existence,
and each of us needs to face each moment,
each passing phase of life with wisdom, acceptance
and compassionate understanding.

If we accept that life is eternal and there are other realms of existence intertwined with our physical world, then it must be a natural step in our evolution to be able to communicate with these other realms and with those who are living on.

Ultimately, mediumistic and spiritual unfoldment are active and evolving paths that lead to new and profound experience and deep communion with the world of the spirit.

Our beginning-less and endless Self
does not need to view life as missed opportunities
but seeks to call us to ways in which it can
skilfully manifest its true nature, its divinity,
more purely in every moment.

Let new knowledge and experience
open you to fresher fields of vision.
For if you wish to develop, what you may think of
as important today may look different to you tomorrow.
This is not to say that what you have so far
discovered and believe to be true is false,
any more than a view from a mountain's peak makes
what is seen from the ground incorrect.

Divinity

10

All life is sacred and ultimately
derives its existence from God.
We therefore need to seek to become one
with this sacredness that exists in everything
and everyone and respect and care for all life,
including ourselves.
Anything that separates us from others
means separating ourselves from life and
the awe inspiring creativity of God and spirit
working through all.

Every living thing and species that exists
is a part of the spirit world.
The natural world is an expression of
the Divine's creation.
And what Nature is, we also are;
for we are also unique parts of Nature
and expressions of divinity.

If at all possible, walk in the fresh air.
Walk where there are trees, where there is Nature,
in a park or forest.
Look for God's presence in the growth of life around you.
Realise that everything is alive in God
and saturated in its divinity,
that you are a part of that divinity and a part of Nature.
As you do so, take a deep breath and
feel your whole self being energised and harmonised
by the vast ocean of life around you.

Take time to look for and experience
God's presence within you and
within the world around you.
Look for it in the setting of a golden sun,
in the sound of a running stream
or in the rustling of leaves in the wind.

I live, move and have my being in the stillness of God.
The light of the supreme Spirit shines through
the whole of my being.
My mind is quiet and receptive to the spirit within.
I am tranquil, calm and at peace with
all my thoughts and with all that surrounds me.

Underlying the wondrous diversity of life
there is one reality
manifesting in an infinite variety of ways.

References

GE *Glyn Edwards (tribute book with material by Glyn)*
Glyn Edwards and other contributors, compiled by Santoshan, 2019

PM *The Potential of Mediumship (expanded edition)*
Glyn Edwards, compiled by Santoshan, 2017

RWG *Realms of Wondrous Gifts (revised edition)*
Santoshan, with conversations with Glyn Edwards, 2018

SG *Spirit Gems (revised edition of 'Unleash Your Spiritual Power and Grow', first published as '21 Steps to Reach Your Spirit')*
Glyn Edwards and Santoshan, 2011

SWPE *The Spirit World in Plain English (revised edition of 'Tune in to Your Spiritual Potential')*
Glyn Edwards and Santoshan, 2011

Note:

Where a quotation appeared in more than one source, the original book it was used in is cited below, except for passages from an article by Glyn called *Intuitive Arts*, which was used in its entirety in *Glyn Edwards: A Renowned Medium Remembered.*

Chapter 1: Awakening

p13 RWG p119
p14 SG p58
p15 SG p95*
p16 SWPE p129*
p17 SG p73
p18 GE p89
p19 PM p69
p20 GE p96
p21 GE p62
p22 SWPE p119*
p23 RWG p126
p24 GE p64
p25 GE p64
p26 SWPE p131*

Chapter 2: The Whole Self

p29 GE p62
p30 PM p116
p31 SG p68
p32 SG p55
p33 SWPE p15
p34 RWG p116

Chapter 3: Growing

p37 SWPE p59*
p38 SWPE p148
p39 PM p63
p40 SG p58
p41 GE p92
p42 GE p64
p43 SWPE p132-133*
p44 GE p74

* *Coauthored by Glyn Edwards and Santoshan (Stephen Wollaston)*

Chapter 4: Unity in Diversity

p47 RWG p126
p48 GE p72
p49 GE p71
p50 SWPE p19*
p51 RWG p123
p52 SWPE p132*
p53 GE p72
p54 GE p68

Chapter 5: Mediumistic Attunement

p57 GE p69
p58 PM p60
p59 PM p61
p60 GE p96
p61 GE p72
p62 GE p92
p63 GE p90
p64 PM p58
p65 GE p87
p66 SWPE p146
p67 PM p24
p68 PM p83
p69 GE p88
p70 GE p95
p71 SG p58
p72 GE p93

Chapter 6: Creativity

p75 RWG p117
p76 PM p91
p77 GE p90
p78 SWPE p15
p79 SG p80
p80 GE p90
p81 PM p92
p82 SWPE p83*

* *Coauthored by Glyn Edwards and Santoshan (Stephen Wollaston)*

Chapter 7: Interconnectedness

p85	GE p64
p86	PM p59
p87	PM p110-111
p88	SWPE p59*
p89	SWPE p120*
p90	GE p62
p91	SG p73
p92	RWG p113
p93	RWG p113
p94	GE p65

Chapter 8: Spirit

p97	GE p64
p98	GE p61
p99	SWPE p142*
p100	PM p29
p101	SG p60
p102	GE p91
p103	PM p119
p104	GE p63
p105	PM p81
p106	SWPE p71*

Chapter 9: Evolving

p109	GE p63
p110	PM p117
p111	RWG p113
p112	SWPE p15
p113	RWG p118
p114	SWPE p133*

Chapter 10: Divinity

p117	SG p73
p118	GE p88-89
p119	SWPE p141*
p120	SWPE p48*
p121	SWPE p46*
p122	SWPE p133*

** Coauthored by Glyn Edwards and Santoshan (Stephen Wollaston)*

About the Compiler

Stephen Wollaston was given the name Santoshan (contentment) by an English swami. He holds a degree in religious studies and a post-graduate certificate in religious education from King's College London. In the late 70s he was the principal bass guitarist of one of London's first punk rock bands, The Wasps. He has been a council member of the UK charity GreenSpirit for many years, is the designer of GreenSpirit magazine, and is an author, coauthor and editor of several books, including *Spirituality Unveiled: Awakening to Creative Life*. He was a close friend of Glyn Edwards for 26 years and worked on a variety of books and projects with him. Currently, he is working towards becoming a OneSpirit Interfaith Foundation minister.

* * *

Glyn Edwards walking between two rows of trees at the Anjali Ashram (a Christian-Indian Ashram that combines aspects of both traditions in its rituals and teachings), Mysore, India. Late December 2009.

'If we look at the early years of modern Spiritualism, we find accounts of spirit communicators bringing not only messages about continuous human progression and survival but also seeking to encourage a recognition of the profound unity we have with all people and all life.'

~ Glyn Edwards, *The Potential of Mediumship (expanded edition)*, p.110.

Other Titles by Glyn Edwards & Santoshan

112 pages
ISBN : 978-0-9569210-4-8

GLYN EDWARDS

A Renowned Medium Remembered
~ Collection of Memories and Teachings
Compiled by Santoshan (Stephen Wollaston)

A unique collection of Glyn's inclusive wisdom on spiritual and mediumistic realms of unfoldment as well as a wonderful tribute book that honours his life and work. In this combined treasury of Glyn's teachings and memories about him, numerous insights and fond recollections are shared alongside various photographs. It includes a detailed biography about him, heartfelt stories by people whose lives he touched, and a collection of quotations, articles, workshop sections and exercises by Glyn, which give practical steps for awakening to the ever-present world of the spirit and the oneness of spiritual living.

'Many people are not aware how outstanding a medium and teacher Glyn in fact was... There are no adequate words to express the void that has been left without his physical presence.'
~ Ron Jordan (Devadūta), internationally renowned medium and spiritual teacher

128 page expanded edition
ISBN 978-0-9569210-3-1

eBook edition available from Barnes & Noble and Smashwords

THE POTENTIAL OF MEDIUMSHIP

A Collection of Essential Teachings and Exercises (expanded edition)
Glyn Edwards
Compiled and with an introduction by Santoshan (Stephen Wollaston)

The Potential of Mediumship presents an inspiring collection of teachings, along with numerous essential exercises for unfolding mediumistic and spiritual gifts. In this first ever anthology of Glyn Edwards's wisdom, he shared first-hand accounts about his own mediumistic experiences and imparted profound insights that will help you to move forward with your abilities. There are chapters here for beginners and the more advanced that reveal how the spirit world can communicate with and work through us and prove survival of life after death.

'There should be many more books like this!'
~ Psychic News

160 pages
ISBN 78-0-9569210-0-0

THE SPIRIT WORLD IN PLAIN ENGLISH

Mediumistic and Spiritual Unfoldment
Glyn Edwards and Santoshan (Stephen Wollaston)
Foreword by Don Hills

The Spirit World in Plain English is a revised and updated edition of the authors' first book. In this beneficial manual, Glyn Edwards and Santoshan share practical exercises and teachings for discovering inherent mediumistic and spiritual potential. Together, they combine their knowledge in far-reaching ways and cover numerous essentials for understanding and interacting with the ever-present world of the spirit.

'This book is more than just another book on spiritual and psychic development; it's literally the bible on development.'
~ Amazon UK (customer review of 1st edition)

144 pages
ISBN 978-1-84694-509-0

SPIRITUALITY UNVEILED

Awakening to Creative Life
Santoshan (Stephen Wollaston)
Foreword by Ian Mowll

Spirituality Unveiled puts forward a succinct and compelling synthesis of numerous spiritual traditions. Whilst weaving together insights from contemporary and past masters of spirituality, along with holistic and Earth centred wisdom, it beautifully highlights teachings about the essentials of creative unfoldment. *Spirituality Unveiled* invites readers to join in the important search to find a healthy interaction with life. Key areas include the power of creativity, the effects of positive and negative actions, and harmonious living with the natural world.

'Integral thinking at its best ... a masterful synthesis.'
~ Marian Van Eyk McCain, editor of *GreenSpirit: Path to a New Consciousness*

'This is a timely book which points a way forward. It also puts God's beautiful creation back at the heart of our relation with the divine."
~ June Raymond, compiler of *Meditations with Thomas Berry* and a sister of Notre Dame.

128 pages
ISBN 978-0-9569210-1-7

SPIRIT GEMS

Essential Guidance for Spiritual, Mediumistic and Creative Unfoldment

Glyn Edwards and Santoshan (Stephen Wollaston)

Spirit Gems is a revised and expanded edition of the authors' second book, which provides practical steps for discovering how to live more freely, deeply and peacefully. Glyn Edwards and Santoshan write beautifully whilst covering essentials such as living in the now, facing our fears, finding unity with all, and harmonising our complete being. Both authors share profound insights for immersing our lives in spiritually-centred living and awakening to the spirit in all. Let their wisdom take you on a journey through various levels of your individual self to omnipresent realms of spirit-life.

'A must for anyone's bookshelf.'
~ The Greater World Newsletter (review of 1st edition)

Low-cost paperback
157 pages
ISBN 978-1723119484

Low-cost eBook edition available from Amazon, Barnes & Noble and Smashwords

REALMS OF WONDROUS GIFTS

Psychic, Mediumistic and Miraculous Powers in the Great Mystical and Wisdom Traditions (revised edition)

Santoshan (Stephen Wollaston)

With conversations with Glyn Edwards

Realms of Wondrous Gifts presents an in-depth look at psychic, mediumistic and miraculous powers in the world's great mystical and wisdom traditions, and includes key insights into various teachings and practices. It also includes two extensive conversations with Glyn Edwards, in which he eloquently shared far-reaching thoughts on several interwoven facets of development.

'A real gem of a book ... Highly recommended.'
~ Psychic World.

'A rare and enriching book.'
~ Eileen Davies, internationally renowned medium and spiritual teacher

86 pages
ISBN 978-0-9935983-2-6

RIVERS OF GREEN WISDOM

Exploring Christian and Yogic Earth Centred Spirituality
Santoshan (Stephen Wollaston)

In *Rivers of Green Wisdom* the author shares personal reflections on Christian, Yogic and Earth centred wisdom and key stages encountered on his own spiritual journey. The book unveils central teachings about the sacredness of Earth and Nature, covers both past and present understanding about our interdependent relationship with the natural world, and how various teachers have looked for East-West fusions for deeper and more responsible living.

'Seldom do you find such practised clarity in revealing the wisdom of Spirit.'
~ Sky McCain, Vedantist and author of *Planet as Self: An Earthen Spirituality*

140 pages
ISBN 978-0-9935983-3-3

The above two books are part of the GreenSpirit Book Series, which is a low-cost series on Gaia-centred spirituality. For more details visit www.greenspirit.org.uk

PATHWAYS OF GREEN WISDOM

Discovering Earth Centred Teachings in Spiritual and Religious Traditions
Edited by Santoshan (Stephen Wollaston)

Pathways of Green Wisdom covers teachings and practices that promote honouring and compassionately caring for Nature. It brings together numerous reflective and informative pieces by contributors to GreenSpirit magazine spanning a period of 11 years, along with especially written new material. Contributors include progressive and insightful writers from various backgrounds. Each offers an enriching well to draw some nourishment and appreciate numerous Earth centred dimensions of a particular spiritual path.

'This is a wonderful book, which takes you on a journey through various traditions.'
~ Ian Mowll, Interfaith minister and the coordinator of GreenSpirit

152 pages
ISBN 978-1986435017

AWAKENING TO EARTH-CENTRED CONSCIOUSNESS

Selection from GreenSpirit Magazine
Edited by Ian Mowll and Santoshan (Stephen Wollaston)

Awakening to Earth-Centred Consciousness shares personal stories, engages thoughtfully with green topics, and provides insightful teachings about our interrelationships with the natural world. It encourages us to embrace an inclusive, compassionate and mindful spirituality – one that leads to interacting with deep levels of life and Nature, of which we are all wondrously interwoven and a part, and the essential obligations this brings for responsible Gaia-centred living.

'A delightful book to dip into for GreenSpirit's existing supporters and a good way to get a feel for GreenSpirit for people who are new to the organisation.'
~ Jane Stott, GreenSpirit council member

124 pages
ISBN 978-1978414716

The above two books are part of the GreenSpirit Book Series, which is a low-cost series on Gaia-centred spirituality. For more details visit www.greenspirit.org.uk

DARK NIGHTS OF THE GREEN SOUL

From Darkness to New Horizons
Edited by Ian Mowll and Santoshan (Stephen Wollaston)

Dark Nights of the Green Soul highlights insights about facing difficult times, alongside reflections on our interactive relationship with Nature. The book's three main parts present various perspectives about working with darkness and ways in which we can creatively move forward. It includes personal stories about times of difficulty people encountered, and explains how each of the storytellers found new meaning and growth by either connecting with an animal friend or in Gaia-centred spiritual awakenings and teachings. The book also reflects upon the state of our planet and offers practical views for the times in which we live and 'the great work' we need to embrace.

***'Dark Nights of the Green Soul* is a compact, intelligent and highly accessible addition to the GreenSpirit Book Series.'**
~ Chris Holmes, GreenSpirit council member

224 pages

ISBN 978-1-846940-24-8

THE HOUSE OF WISDOM

Yoga Spirituality of the East and West

Swami Dharmananda Saraswati and Santoshan (Stephen Wollaston)

Foreword by Glyn Edwards

The House of Wisdom covers starting out on the spiritual path, the challenges along the way, and the Yogic understanding of the authentic Self. It looks closely at the Yogic tradition and includes various exercises and practices for relaxation and discovering and harmonising the spiritual whole of ourselves.

'An excellent book ... a real treasure-house of spiritual knowledge.'

~ Julie Friedeberger, author of *The Healing Power of Yoga*

AUDIO CDs BY AND DOWNLOADS OF GLYN EDWARDS

Audio CDs by Glyn Edwards available from the Mind-Body-Spirit Online website:

www.mindbodyspiritonline.co.uk

Tel: (01202) 267684 (outside UK: +441202 267684)

Downloads of CDs by Glyn Edwards available from:

www.listening2spirit.com

Mind-Body-Spirit Online are also the main stockist of books by Glyn Edwards

---

Glyn Edwards remembered website:

https://glynedwards.wixsite.com/glynedwards

46067134R00082

Printed in Poland
by Amazon Fulfillment
Poland Sp. z o.o., Wrocław